Wellspring
PRESS

ISBN: 978-1-956334-03-6

# Important Information

| | |
|---|---|
| Property Address | |
| Property Phone Number | |
| Property Management/ Owner Contact Information | |
| Internet/Cable Provider | |
| WIFI Network | |
| WIFI Password | |
| Hospital | |
| Urgent Care | |
| Grocery Store(s) | |
| | |
| Water Sports Rental *(jet ski, boats, etc.)* | |
| | |

# Our Local Favorites

| | |
|---|---|
| Pizza | |
| Food Delivery Services | |
| Dine-In Restaurant(s) | |
| Activities | |
| Sightseeing | |
| Attractions | |

# Miscellaneous Information

|  |  |
|--|--|
|  |  |
|  |  |
|  |  |
|  |  |
|  |  |
|  |  |
|  |  |
|  |  |

# Miscellaneous Information

|  |  |
|---|---|
|  |  |
|  |  |
|  |  |
|  |  |
|  |  |
|  |  |
|  |  |
|  |  |
|  |  |

Our Message for You...

| | |
|---|---|
| Dates of Stay | |
| Visitor Name(s) | |
| Visiting From | |
| | |

We would love to hear about your stay. Please share your favorite places, memories, activities and experiences. We hope you had a wonderful time and come back to visit again soon!

| |
|---|
| |
| |
| |
| |
| |
| |
| |
| |
| |
| |
| |
| |
| May we share your testimonial? _____ Yes _____ No |

| | |
|---|---|
| Dates of Stay | |
| Visitor Name(s) | |
| Visiting From | |
| | |

We would love to hear about your stay. Please share your favorite places, memories, activities and experiences. We hope you had a wonderful time and come back to visit again soon!

May we share your testimonial? _____ Yes _____ No

| Dates of Stay | |
| --- | --- |
| Visitor Name(s) | |
| Visiting From | |
| | |

We would love to hear about your stay. Please share your favorite places, memories, activities and experiences. We hope you had a wonderful time and come back to visit again soon!

May we share your testimonial? _____ Yes _____ No

| | |
|---|---|
| Dates of Stay | |
| Visitor Name(s) | |
| Visiting From | |
| | |

We would love to hear about your stay. Please share your favorite places, memories, activities and experiences. We hope you had a wonderful time and come back to visit again soon!

May we share your testimonial? _____ Yes _____ No

| Dates of Stay | |
| --- | --- |
| Visitor Name(s) | |
| Visiting From | |
| | |

We would love to hear about your stay. Please share your favorite places, memories, activities and experiences. We hope you had a wonderful time and come back to visit again soon!

May we share your testimonial? _____ Yes _____ No

| | |
|---|---|
| Dates of Stay | |
| Visitor Name(s) | |
| Visiting From | |
| | |

We would love to hear about your stay. Please share your favorite places, memories, activities and experiences. We hope you had a wonderful time and come back to visit again soon!

May we share your testimonial? _____ Yes _____ No

| | |
|---|---|
| Dates of Stay | |
| Visitor Name(s) | |
| Visiting From | |
| | |

We would love to hear about your stay. Please share your favorite places, memories, activities and experiences. We hope you had a wonderful time and come back to visit again soon!

May we share your testimonial? _____ Yes _____ No

| | |
|---|---|
| Dates of Stay | |
| Visitor Name(s) | |
| Visiting From | |
| | |

We would love to hear about your stay. Please share your favorite places, memories, activities and experiences. We hope you had a wonderful time and come back to visit again soon!

May we share your testimonial? _____ Yes _____ No

| | |
|---|---|
| Dates of Stay | |
| Visitor Name(s) | |
| Visiting From | |
| | |

We would love to hear about your stay. Please share your favorite places, memories, activities and experiences. We hope you had a wonderful time and come back to visit again soon!

May we share your testimonial? _____ Yes _____ No

| | |
|---|---|
| Dates of Stay | |
| Visitor Name(s) | |
| Visiting From | |
| | |

We would love to hear about your stay. Please share your favorite places, memories, activities and experiences. We hope you had a wonderful time and come back to visit again soon!

May we share your testimonial? _____Yes _____No

| | |
|---|---|
| Dates of Stay | |
| Visitor Name(s) | |
| Visiting From | |
| | |

We would love to hear about your stay. Please share your favorite places, memories, activities and experiences. We hope you had a wonderful time and come back to visit again soon!

May we share your testimonial? _____ Yes _____ No

| Dates of Stay | |
|---|---|
| Visitor Name(s) | |
| Visiting From | |
| | |

We would love to hear about your stay. Please share your favorite places, memories, activities and experiences. We hope you had a wonderful time and come back to visit again soon!

|  |
|---|
|  |
|  |
|  |
|  |
|  |
|  |
|  |
|  |
|  |
|  |
|  |
|  |
|  |

May we share your testimonial? _____ Yes _____ No

| | |
|---|---|
| Dates of Stay | |
| Visitor Name(s) | |
| Visiting From | |
| | |

We would love to hear about your stay. Please share your favorite places, memories, activities and experiences. We hope you had a wonderful time and come back to visit again soon!

May we share your testimonial? _____ Yes _____ No

| | |
|---|---|
| Dates of Stay | |
| Visitor Name(s) | |
| Visiting From | |
| | |

We would love to hear about your stay. Please share your favorite places, memories, activities and experiences. We hope you had a wonderful time and come back to visit again soon!

May we share your testimonial? _____ Yes _____ No

| | |
|---|---|
| Dates of Stay | |
| Visitor Name(s) | |
| Visiting From | |
| | |

We would love to hear about your stay. Please share your favorite places, memories, activities and experiences. We hope you had a wonderful time and come back to visit again soon!

May we share your testimonial? _____ Yes _____ No

| | |
|---|---|
| Dates of Stay | |
| Visitor Name(s) | |
| Visiting From | |
| | |

We would love to hear about your stay.  Please share your favorite places, memories, activities and experiences.  We hope you had a wonderful time and come back to visit again soon!

May we share your testimonial? _____Yes _____No

| Dates of Stay | |
|---|---|
| Visitor Name(s) | |
| Visiting From | |
| | |

We would love to hear about your stay. Please share your favorite places, memories, activities and experiences. We hope you had a wonderful time and come back to visit again soon!

May we share your testimonial? _____ Yes _____ No

| | |
|---|---|
| Dates of Stay | |
| Visitor Name(s) | |
| Visiting From | |
| | |

We would love to hear about your stay.  Please share your favorite places, memories, activities and experiences.  We hope you had a wonderful time and come back to visit again soon!

May we share your testimonial?  _____ Yes _____ No

| | |
|---|---|
| Dates of Stay | |
| Visitor Name(s) | |
| Visiting From | |
| | |

We would love to hear about your stay.  Please share your favorite places, memories, activities and experiences.  We hope you had a wonderful time and come back to visit again soon!

May we share your testimonial? _____Yes _____No

| | |
|---|---|
| Dates of Stay | |
| Visitor Name(s) | |
| Visiting From | |
| | |

We would love to hear about your stay. Please share your favorite places, memories, activities and experiences. We hope you had a wonderful time and come back to visit again soon!

May we share your testimonial? _____ Yes _____ No

| Dates of Stay | |
| --- | --- |
| Visitor Name(s) | |
| Visiting From | |
| | |

We would love to hear about your stay. Please share your favorite places, memories, activities and experiences. We hope you had a wonderful time and come back to visit again soon!

May we share your testimonial? _____ Yes _____ No

| | |
|---|---|
| Dates of Stay | |
| Visitor Name(s) | |
| Visiting From | |
| | |

We would love to hear about your stay. Please share your favorite places, memories, activities and experiences. We hope you had a wonderful time and come back to visit again soon!

May we share your testimonial? _____ Yes _____ No

| | |
|---|---|
| Dates of Stay | |
| Visitor Name(s) | |
| Visiting From | |
| | |

We would love to hear about your stay. Please share your favorite places, memories, activities and experiences. We hope you had a wonderful time and come back to visit again soon!

May we share your testimonial? _____ Yes _____ No

| | |
|---|---|
| Dates of Stay | |
| Visitor Name(s) | |
| Visiting From | |
| | |

We would love to hear about your stay. Please share your favorite places, memories, activities and experiences. We hope you had a wonderful time and come back to visit again soon!

May we share your testimonial? _____ Yes _____ No

| | |
|---|---|
| Dates of Stay | |
| Visitor Name(s) | |
| Visiting From | |
| | |

We would love to hear about your stay. Please share your favorite places, memories, activities and experiences. We hope you had a wonderful time and come back to visit again soon!

| |
|---|
| |
| |
| |
| |
| |
| |
| |
| |
| |
| |
| |
| |
| May we share your testimonial? _____ Yes _____ No |

| Dates of Stay | |
| --- | --- |
| Visitor Name(s) | |
| Visiting From | |
| | |

We would love to hear about your stay. Please share your favorite places, memories, activities and experiences. We hope you had a wonderful time and come back to visit again soon!

May we share your testimonial? _____Yes _____No

| Dates of Stay | |
|---|---|
| Visitor Name(s) | |
| Visiting From | |
| | |

We would love to hear about your stay. Please share your favorite places, memories, activities and experiences. We hope you had a wonderful time and come back to visit again soon!

|  |
|---|
|  |
|  |
|  |
|  |
|  |
|  |
|  |
|  |
|  |
|  |
|  |
|  |
| May we share your testimonial? _____ Yes _____ No |

| | |
|---|---|
| Dates of Stay | |
| Visitor Name(s) | |
| Visiting From | |
| | |

We would love to hear about your stay. Please share your favorite places, memories, activities and experiences. We hope you had a wonderful time and come back to visit again soon!

May we share your testimonial? _____ Yes _____ No

| | |
|---|---|
| Dates of Stay | |
| Visitor Name(s) | |
| Visiting From | |
| | |

We would love to hear about your stay. Please share your favorite places, memories, activities and experiences. We hope you had a wonderful time and come back to visit again soon!

May we share your testimonial? _____ Yes _____ No

| | |
|---|---|
| Dates of Stay | |
| Visitor Name(s) | |
| Visiting From | |
| | |

We would love to hear about your stay. Please share your favorite places, memories, activities and experiences. We hope you had a wonderful time and come back to visit again soon!

May we share your testimonial? _____ Yes _____ No

| | |
|---|---|
| Dates of Stay | |
| Visitor Name(s) | |
| Visiting From | |
| | |

We would love to hear about your stay.  Please share your favorite places, memories, activities and experiences.  We hope you had a wonderful time and come back to visit again soon!

| |
|---|
| |
| |
| |
| |
| |
| |
| |
| |
| |
| |
| |
| |
| |
| May we share your testimonial? _____ Yes _____ No |

| | |
|---|---|
| Dates of Stay | |
| Visitor Name(s) | |
| Visiting From | |
| | |

We would love to hear about your stay. Please share your favorite places, memories, activities and experiences. We hope you had a wonderful time and come back to visit again soon!

May we share your testimonial? _____ Yes _____ No

| | |
|---|---|
| Dates of Stay | |
| Visitor Name(s) | |
| Visiting From | |
| | |

We would love to hear about your stay. Please share your favorite places, memories, activities and experiences. We hope you had a wonderful time and come back to visit again soon!

|  |
|---|
|  |
|  |
|  |
|  |
|  |
|  |
|  |
|  |
|  |
|  |
|  |
|  |
| May we share your testimonial? _____Yes _____No |

| | |
|---|---|
| Dates of Stay | |
| Visitor Name(s) | |
| Visiting From | |
| | |

We would love to hear about your stay. Please share your favorite places, memories, activities and experiences. We hope you had a wonderful time and come back to visit again soon!

May we share your testimonial? _____Yes _____No

| | |
|---|---|
| Dates of Stay | |
| Visitor Name(s) | |
| Visiting From | |
| | |

We would love to hear about your stay. Please share your favorite places, memories, activities and experiences. We hope you had a wonderful time and come back to visit again soon!

May we share your testimonial? _____ Yes _____ No

| | |
|---|---|
| Dates of Stay | |
| Visitor Name(s) | |
| Visiting From | |
| | |

We would love to hear about your stay. Please share your favorite places, memories, activities and experiences. We hope you had a wonderful time and come back to visit again soon!

May we share your testimonial? _____ Yes _____ No

| | |
|---|---|
| Dates of Stay | |
| Visitor Name(s) | |
| Visiting From | |
| | |

We would love to hear about your stay. Please share your favorite places, memories, activities and experiences. We hope you had a wonderful time and come back to visit again soon!

| |
|---|
| |
| |
| |
| |
| |
| |
| |
| |
| |
| |
| |
| |
| May we share your testimonial? _____ Yes _____ No |

| Dates of Stay | |
| --- | --- |
| Visitor Name(s) | |
| Visiting From | |
| | |

We would love to hear about your stay. Please share your favorite places, memories, activities and experiences. We hope you had a wonderful time and come back to visit again soon!

May we share your testimonial? _____ Yes _____ No

| | |
|---|---|
| Dates of Stay | |
| Visitor Name(s) | |
| Visiting From | |
| | |

We would love to hear about your stay. Please share your favorite places, memories, activities and experiences. We hope you had a wonderful time and come back to visit again soon!

May we share your testimonial? _____ Yes _____ No

| | |
|---|---|
| Dates of Stay | |
| Visitor Name(s) | |
| Visiting From | |
| | |

We would love to hear about your stay. Please share your favorite places, memories, activities and experiences. We hope you had a wonderful time and come back to visit again soon!

May we share your testimonial? _____ Yes _____ No

| | |
|---|---|
| Dates of Stay | |
| Visitor Name(s) | |
| Visiting From | |
| | |

We would love to hear about your stay. Please share your favorite places, memories, activities and experiences. We hope you had a wonderful time and come back to visit again soon!

May we share your testimonial? _____ Yes _____ No

| Dates of Stay | |
| --- | --- |
| Visitor Name(s) | |
| Visiting From | |
| | |

We would love to hear about your stay. Please share your favorite places, memories, activities and experiences. We hope you had a wonderful time and come back to visit again soon!

May we share your testimonial? _____ Yes _____ No

| | |
|---|---|
| Dates of Stay | |
| Visitor Name(s) | |
| Visiting From | |
| | |

We would love to hear about your stay. Please share your favorite places, memories, activities and experiences. We hope you had a wonderful time and come back to visit again soon!

| |
|---|
| |
| |
| |
| |
| |
| |
| |
| |
| |
| |
| |
| |
| May we share your testimonial? _____ Yes _____ No |

| Dates of Stay | |
|---|---|
| Visitor Name(s) | |
| Visiting From | |
| | |

We would love to hear about your stay. Please share your favorite places, memories, activities and experiences. We hope you had a wonderful time and come back to visit again soon!

May we share your testimonial? _____ Yes _____ No

| | |
|---|---|
| Dates of Stay | |
| Visitor Name(s) | |
| Visiting From | |
| | |

We would love to hear about your stay. Please share your favorite places, memories, activities and experiences. We hope you had a wonderful time and come back to visit again soon!

May we share your testimonial? _____ Yes _____ No

| | |
|---|---|
| Dates of Stay | |
| Visitor Name(s) | |
| Visiting From | |
| | |

We would love to hear about your stay. Please share your favorite places, memories, activities and experiences. We hope you had a wonderful time and come back to visit again soon!

May we share your testimonial? _____ Yes _____ No

| | |
|---|---|
| Dates of Stay | |
| Visitor Name(s) | |
| Visiting From | |
| | |

We would love to hear about your stay. Please share your favorite places, memories, activities and experiences. We hope you had a wonderful time and come back to visit again soon!

| |
|---|
| |
| |
| |
| |
| |
| |
| |
| |
| |
| |
| |
| |
| May we share your testimonial? _____ Yes _____ No |

| Dates of Stay | |
|---|---|
| Visitor Name(s) | |
| Visiting From | |
| | |

We would love to hear about your stay. Please share your favorite places, memories, activities and experiences. We hope you had a wonderful time and come back to visit again soon!

| |
|---|
| |
| |
| |
| |
| |
| |
| |
| |
| |
| |
| |
| |
| |
| May we share your testimonial? _____ Yes _____ No |

| | |
|---|---|
| Dates of Stay | |
| Visitor Name(s) | |
| Visiting From | |
| | |

We would love to hear about your stay. Please share your favorite places, memories, activities and experiences. We hope you had a wonderful time and come back to visit again soon!

| | |
|---|---|
| Dates of Stay | |
| Visitor Name(s) | |
| Visiting From | |
| | |

We would love to hear about your stay. Please share your favorite places, memories, activities and experiences. We hope you had a wonderful time and come back to visit again soon!

May we share your testimonial? _____ Yes _____ No

| Dates of Stay | |
|---|---|
| Visitor Name(s) | |
| Visiting From | |
| | |

We would love to hear about your stay. Please share your favorite places, memories, activities and experiences. We hope you had a wonderful time and come back to visit again soon!

| |
|---|
| |
| |
| |
| |
| |
| |
| |
| |
| |
| |
| |
| |
| |
| May we share your testimonial? _____ Yes _____ No |

| | |
|---|---|
| Dates of Stay | |
| Visitor Name(s) | |
| Visiting From | |
| | |

We would love to hear about your stay. Please share your favorite places, memories, activities and experiences. We hope you had a wonderful time and come back to visit again soon!

May we share your testimonial? _____Yes _____No

| Dates of Stay | |
| --- | --- |
| Visitor Name(s) | |
| Visiting From | |
| | |

We would love to hear about your stay. Please share your
favorite places, memories, activities and experiences. We hope
you had a wonderful time and come back to visit again soon!

|  |
| --- |
|  |
|  |
|  |
|  |
|  |
|  |
|  |
|  |
|  |
|  |
|  |
|  |
| May we share your testimonial? _____ Yes _____ No |

| Dates of Stay | |
|---|---|
| Visitor Name(s) | |
| Visiting From | |
| | |

We would love to hear about your stay. Please share your favorite places, memories, activities and experiences. We hope you had a wonderful time and come back to visit again soon!

May we share your testimonial? _____ Yes _____ No

| | |
|---|---|
| Dates of Stay | |
| Visitor Name(s) | |
| Visiting From | |
| | |

We would love to hear about your stay. Please share your favorite places, memories, activities and experiences. We hope you had a wonderful time and come back to visit again soon!

May we share your testimonial? _____ Yes _____ No

| | |
|---|---|
| Dates of Stay | |
| Visitor Name(s) | |
| Visiting From | |
| | |

We would love to hear about your stay. Please share your favorite places, memories, activities and experiences. We hope you had a wonderful time and come back to visit again soon!

May we share your testimonial? _____ Yes _____ No

| | |
|---|---|
| Dates of Stay | |
| Visitor Name(s) | |
| Visiting From | |
| | |

We would love to hear about your stay. Please share your favorite places, memories, activities and experiences. We hope you had a wonderful time and come back to visit again soon!

May we share your testimonial? _____ Yes _____ No

| | |
|---|---|
| Dates of Stay | |
| Visitor Name(s) | |
| Visiting From | |
| | |

We would love to hear about your stay. Please share your favorite places, memories, activities and experiences. We hope you had a wonderful time and come back to visit again soon!

May we share your testimonial? _____ Yes _____ No

| | |
|---|---|
| Dates of Stay | |
| Visitor Name(s) | |
| Visiting From | |
| | |

We would love to hear about your stay. Please share your favorite places, memories, activities and experiences. We hope you had a wonderful time and come back to visit again soon!

May we share your testimonial? _____ Yes _____ No

| Dates of Stay | |
|---|---|
| Visitor Name(s) | |
| Visiting From | |
| | |

We would love to hear about your stay. Please share your favorite places, memories, activities and experiences. We hope you had a wonderful time and come back to visit again soon!

May we share your testimonial? _____ Yes _____ No

| | |
|---|---|
| Dates of Stay | |
| Visitor Name(s) | |
| Visiting From | |
| | |

We would love to hear about your stay. Please share your favorite places, memories, activities and experiences. We hope you had a wonderful time and come back to visit again soon!

May we share your testimonial? _____Yes _____No

| Dates of Stay | |
|---|---|
| Visitor Name(s) | |
| Visiting From | |
| | |

We would love to hear about your stay. Please share your
favorite places, memories, activities and experiences. We hope
you had a wonderful time and come back to visit again soon!

| |
|---|
| |
| |
| |
| |
| |
| |
| |
| |
| |
| |
| |
| |
| May we share your testimonial? _____Yes _____No |

| | |
|---|---|
| Dates of Stay | |
| Visitor Name(s) | |
| Visiting From | |
| | |

We would love to hear about your stay. Please share your favorite places, memories, activities and experiences. We hope you had a wonderful time and come back to visit again soon!

May we share your testimonial? _____ Yes _____ No

| Dates of Stay | |
|---|---|
| Visitor Name(s) | |
| Visiting From | |
| | |

We would love to hear about your stay. Please share your favorite places, memories, activities and experiences. We hope you had a wonderful time and come back to visit again soon!

May we share your testimonial? _____Yes _____No

| | |
|---|---|
| Dates of Stay | |
| Visitor Name(s) | |
| Visiting From | |
| | |

We would love to hear about your stay. Please share your favorite places, memories, activities and experiences. We hope you had a wonderful time and come back to visit again soon!

May we share your testimonial? _____ Yes _____ No

| | |
|---|---|
| Dates of Stay | |
| Visitor Name(s) | |
| Visiting From | |
| | |

We would love to hear about your stay. Please share your favorite places, memories, activities and experiences. We hope you had a wonderful time and come back to visit again soon!

May we share your testimonial? _____ Yes _____ No

| Dates of Stay | |
|---|---|
| Visitor Name(s) | |
| Visiting From | |
| | |

We would love to hear about your stay. Please share your favorite places, memories, activities and experiences. We hope you had a wonderful time and come back to visit again soon!

| |
|---|
| |
| |
| |
| |
| |
| |
| |
| |
| |
| |
| |
| May we share your testimonial? _____ Yes _____ No |

| | |
|---|---|
| Dates of Stay | |
| Visitor Name(s) | |
| Visiting From | |
| | |

We would love to hear about your stay. Please share your favorite places, memories, activities and experiences. We hope you had a wonderful time and come back to visit again soon!

May we share your testimonial? _____ Yes _____ No

| Dates of Stay | |
|---|---|
| Visitor Name(s) | |
| Visiting From | |
| | |

We would love to hear about your stay. Please share your favorite places, memories, activities and experiences. We hope you had a wonderful time and come back to visit again soon!

May we share your testimonial? _____ Yes _____ No

| | |
|---|---|
| Dates of Stay | |
| Visitor Name(s) | |
| Visiting From | |
| | |

We would love to hear about your stay. Please share your favorite places, memories, activities and experiences. We hope you had a wonderful time and come back to visit again soon!

May we share your testimonial? _____ Yes _____ No

| Dates of Stay | |
| --- | --- |
| Visitor Name(s) | |
| Visiting From | |
| | |

We would love to hear about your stay. Please share your favorite places, memories, activities and experiences. We hope you had a wonderful time and come back to visit again soon!

May we share your testimonial? _____ Yes _____ No

| | |
|---|---|
| Dates of Stay | |
| Visitor Name(s) | |
| Visiting From | |
| | |

We would love to hear about your stay. Please share your favorite places, memories, activities and experiences. We hope you had a wonderful time and come back to visit again soon!

May we share your testimonial? _____ Yes _____ No

| | |
|---|---|
| Dates of Stay | |
| Visitor Name(s) | |
| Visiting From | |
| | |

We would love to hear about your stay. Please share your favorite places, memories, activities and experiences. We hope you had a wonderful time and come back to visit again soon!

| |
|---|
| |
| |
| |
| |
| |
| |
| |
| |
| |
| |
| |
| |
| May we share your testimonial? _____ Yes _____ No |

| | |
|---|---|
| Dates of Stay | |
| Visitor Name(s) | |
| Visiting From | |
| | |

We would love to hear about your stay. Please share your favorite places, memories, activities and experiences. We hope you had a wonderful time and come back to visit again soon!

May we share your testimonial? _____Yes _____No

| | |
|---|---|
| Dates of Stay | |
| Visitor Name(s) | |
| Visiting From | |
| | |

We would love to hear about your stay. Please share your favorite places, memories, activities and experiences. We hope you had a wonderful time and come back to visit again soon!

May we share your testimonial? _____ Yes _____ No

| | |
|---|---|
| Dates of Stay | |
| Visitor Name(s) | |
| Visiting From | |
| | |

We would love to hear about your stay. Please share your favorite places, memories, activities and experiences. We hope you had a wonderful time and come back to visit again soon!

May we share your testimonial? _____ Yes _____ No

| | |
|---|---|
| Dates of Stay | |
| Visitor Name(s) | |
| Visiting From | |
| | |

We would love to hear about your stay.  Please share your favorite places, memories, activities and experiences.  We hope you had a wonderful time and come back to visit again soon!

May we share your testimonial? _____ Yes _____ No

| Dates of Stay | |
| --- | --- |
| Visitor Name(s) | |
| Visiting From | |
| | |

We would love to hear about your stay. Please share your favorite places, memories, activities and experiences. We hope you had a wonderful time and come back to visit again soon!

May we share your testimonial? _____ Yes _____ No

| Dates of Stay | |
|---|---|
| Visitor Name(s) | |
| Visiting From | |
| | |

We would love to hear about your stay. Please share your favorite places, memories, activities and experiences. We hope you had a wonderful time and come back to visit again soon!

|  |
|---|
|  |
|  |
|  |
|  |
|  |
|  |
|  |
|  |
|  |
|  |
|  |
|  |
|  |

May we share your testimonial? _____ Yes _____ No

| Dates of Stay | |
|---|---|
| Visitor Name(s) | |
| Visiting From | |
| | |

We would love to hear about your stay. Please share your favorite places, memories, activities and experiences. We hope you had a wonderful time and come back to visit again soon!

May we share your testimonial? _____ Yes _____ No

| | |
|---|---|
| Dates of Stay | |
| Visitor Name(s) | |
| Visiting From | |
| | |

We would love to hear about your stay. Please share your favorite places, memories, activities and experiences. We hope you had a wonderful time and come back to visit again soon!

May we share your testimonial? _____ Yes _____ No

| | |
|---|---|
| Dates of Stay | |
| Visitor Name(s) | |
| Visiting From | |
| | |

We would love to hear about your stay. Please share your favorite places, memories, activities and experiences. We hope you had a wonderful time and come back to visit again soon!

May we share your testimonial? _____ Yes _____ No

| | |
|---|---|
| Dates of Stay | |
| Visitor Name(s) | |
| Visiting From | |
| | |

We would love to hear about your stay. Please share your favorite places, memories, activities and experiences. We hope you had a wonderful time and come back to visit again soon!

| |
|---|
| |
| |
| |
| |
| |
| |
| |
| |
| |
| |
| |
| |
| |
| May we share your testimonial? _____ Yes _____ No |

| Dates of Stay | |
| --- | --- |
| Visitor Name(s) | |
| Visiting From | |
| | |

We would love to hear about your stay. Please share your favorite places, memories, activities and experiences. We hope you had a wonderful time and come back to visit again soon!

May we share your testimonial? _____Yes _____No

| | |
|---|---|
| Dates of Stay | |
| Visitor Name(s) | |
| Visiting From | |
| | |

We would love to hear about your stay.  Please share your favorite places, memories, activities and experiences.  We hope you had a wonderful time and come back to visit again soon!

May we share your testimonial? _____ Yes _____ No

| Dates of Stay | |
|---|---|
| Visitor Name(s) | |
| Visiting From | |
| | |

We would love to hear about your stay. Please share your favorite places, memories, activities and experiences. We hope you had a wonderful time and come back to visit again soon!

May we share your testimonial? _____ Yes _____ No

| | |
|---|---|
| Dates of Stay | |
| Visitor Name(s) | |
| Visiting From | |
| | |

We would love to hear about your stay. Please share your favorite places, memories, activities and experiences. We hope you had a wonderful time and come back to visit again soon!

May we share your testimonial? _____ Yes _____ No

| Dates of Stay | |
| --- | --- |
| Visitor Name(s) | |
| Visiting From | |
| | |

We would love to hear about your stay. Please share your favorite places, memories, activities and experiences. We hope you had a wonderful time and come back to visit again soon!

May we share your testimonial? _____Yes _____No

| | |
|---|---|
| Dates of Stay | |
| Visitor Name(s) | |
| Visiting From | |
| | |

We would love to hear about your stay. Please share your favorite places, memories, activities and experiences. We hope you had a wonderful time and come back to visit again soon!

May we share your testimonial? _____ Yes _____ No

| | |
|---|---|
| Dates of Stay | |
| Visitor Name(s) | |
| Visiting From | |
| | |

We would love to hear about your stay. Please share your favorite places, memories, activities and experiences. We hope you had a wonderful time and come back to visit again soon!

May we share your testimonial? _____ Yes _____ No

| | |
|---|---|
| Dates of Stay | |
| Visitor Name(s) | |
| Visiting From | |
| | |

We would love to hear about your stay. Please share your favorite places, memories, activities and experiences. We hope you had a wonderful time and come back to visit again soon!

| |
|---|
| |
| |
| |
| |
| |
| |
| |
| |
| |
| |
| |
| |
| May we share your testimonial? _____ Yes _____ No |

| Dates of Stay | |
| --- | --- |
| Visitor Name(s) | |
| Visiting From | |
| | |

We would love to hear about your stay. Please share your favorite places, memories, activities and experiences. We hope you had a wonderful time and come back to visit again soon!

May we share your testimonial? _____ Yes _____ No

| | |
|---|---|
| Dates of Stay | |
| Visitor Name(s) | |
| Visiting From | |
| | |

We would love to hear about your stay. Please share your favorite places, memories, activities and experiences. We hope you had a wonderful time and come back to visit again soon!

May we share your testimonial? _____ Yes _____ No

| Dates of Stay | |
|---|---|
| Visitor Name(s) | |
| Visiting From | |
| | |

We would love to hear about your stay. Please share your favorite places, memories, activities and experiences. We hope you had a wonderful time and come back to visit again soon!

May we share your testimonial? _____Yes _____No

| | |
|---|---|
| Dates of Stay | |
| Visitor Name(s) | |
| Visiting From | |
| | |

We would love to hear about your stay. Please share your favorite places, memories, activities and experiences. We hope you had a wonderful time and come back to visit again soon!

May we share your testimonial? _____ Yes _____ No

| | |
|---|---|
| Dates of Stay | |
| Visitor Name(s) | |
| Visiting From | |
| | |

We would love to hear about your stay. Please share your favorite places, memories, activities and experiences. We hope you had a wonderful time and come back to visit again soon!

May we share your testimonial? _____ Yes _____ No

| | |
|---|---|
| Dates of Stay | |
| Visitor Name(s) | |
| Visiting From | |
| | |

We would love to hear about your stay. Please share your favorite places, memories, activities and experiences. We hope you had a wonderful time and come back to visit again soon!

May we share your testimonial? _____ Yes _____ No

| | |
|---|---|
| Dates of Stay | |
| Visitor Name(s) | |
| Visiting From | |
| | |

We would love to hear about your stay. Please share your favorite places, memories, activities and experiences. We hope you had a wonderful time and come back to visit again soon!

| |
|---|
| |
| |
| |
| |
| |
| |
| |
| |
| |
| |
| |
| |
| |
| May we share your testimonial? _____ Yes _____ No |

| Dates of Stay | |
|---|---|
| Visitor Name(s) | |
| Visiting From | |
| | |

We would love to hear about your stay. Please share your favorite places, memories, activities and experiences. We hope you had a wonderful time and come back to visit again soon!

May we share your testimonial? _____ Yes _____ No

| | |
|---|---|
| Dates of Stay | |
| Visitor Name(s) | |
| Visiting From | |
| | |

We would love to hear about your stay. Please share your favorite places, memories, activities and experiences. We hope you had a wonderful time and come back to visit again soon!

May we share your testimonial? _____Yes _____No

| Dates of Stay | |
|---|---|
| Visitor Name(s) | |
| Visiting From | |
| | |

We would love to hear about your stay. Please share your favorite places, memories, activities and experiences. We hope you had a wonderful time and come back to visit again soon!

| |
|---|
| |
| |
| |
| |
| |
| |
| |
| |
| |
| |
| |
| |
| May we share your testimonial? _____ Yes _____ No |

| Dates of Stay | |
| --- | --- |
| Visitor Name(s) | |
| Visiting From | |
| | |

We would love to hear about your stay. Please share your favorite places, memories, activities and experiences. We hope you had a wonderful time and come back to visit again soon!

May we share your testimonial? _____ Yes _____ No

| Dates of Stay | |
|---|---|
| Visitor Name(s) | |
| Visiting From | |
| | |

We would love to hear about your stay. Please share your favorite places, memories, activities and experiences. We hope you had a wonderful time and come back to visit again soon!

|  |
|---|
|  |
|  |
|  |
|  |
|  |
|  |
|  |
|  |
|  |
|  |
|  |
|  |
|  |
| May we share your testimonial? _____ Yes _____ No |

| | |
|---|---|
| Dates of Stay | |
| Visitor Name(s) | |
| Visiting From | |
| | |

We would love to hear about your stay. Please share your favorite places, memories, activities and experiences. We hope you had a wonderful time and come back to visit again soon!

May we share your testimonial? _____ Yes _____ No

| Dates of Stay | |
|---|---|
| Visitor Name(s) | |
| Visiting From | |
| | |

We would love to hear about your stay. Please share your favorite places, memories, activities and experiences. We hope you had a wonderful time and come back to visit again soon!

May we share your testimonial? _____ Yes _____ No

| | |
|---|---|
| Dates of Stay | |
| Visitor Name(s) | |
| Visiting From | |
| | |

We would love to hear about your stay. Please share your favorite places, memories, activities and experiences. We hope you had a wonderful time and come back to visit again soon!

May we share your testimonial? _____ Yes _____ No

| Dates of Stay | |
| --- | --- |
| Visitor Name(s) | |
| Visiting From | |
| | |

We would love to hear about your stay. Please share your favorite places, memories, activities and experiences. We hope you had a wonderful time and come back to visit again soon!

| |
| --- |
| |
| |
| |
| |
| |
| |
| |
| |
| |
| |
| |
| |
| |
| |
| May we share your testimonial? _____ Yes _____ No |

| | |
|---|---|
| Dates of Stay | |
| Visitor Name(s) | |
| Visiting From | |
| | |

We would love to hear about your stay. Please share your favorite places, memories, activities and experiences. We hope you had a wonderful time and come back to visit again soon!

May we share your testimonial? _____ Yes _____ No

| | |
|---|---|
| Dates of Stay | |
| Visitor Name(s) | |
| Visiting From | |
| | |

We would love to hear about your stay. Please share your favorite places, memories, activities and experiences. We hope you had a wonderful time and come back to visit again soon!

May we share your testimonial? _____ Yes _____ No

| | |
|---|---|
| Dates of Stay | |
| Visitor Name(s) | |
| Visiting From | |
| | |

We would love to hear about your stay. Please share your favorite places, memories, activities and experiences. We hope you had a wonderful time and come back to visit again soon!

May we share your testimonial? _____ Yes _____ No

| | |
|---|---|
| Dates of Stay | |
| Visitor Name(s) | |
| Visiting From | |
| | |

We would love to hear about your stay. Please share your favorite places, memories, activities and experiences. We hope you had a wonderful time and come back to visit again soon!

May we share your testimonial? _____ Yes _____ No

| | |
|---|---|
| Dates of Stay | |
| Visitor Name(s) | |
| Visiting From | |
| | |

We would love to hear about your stay. Please share your favorite places, memories, activities and experiences. We hope you had a wonderful time and come back to visit again soon!

May we share your testimonial? _____ Yes _____ No

www.ingramcontent.com/pod-product-compliance
Lightning Source LLC
Chambersburg PA
CBHW060813100426
42813CB00004B/1055

* 9 7 8 1 9 5 6 3 3 4 0 3 6 *